Brexit:
Age of Boris Johnson

Written by:
Ovidijus Gelzinis

Contents

Chapter 1: Greece vs Rome

In November of 2015, the then Mayor of London Boris Johnson debated the famous scholar Mary Beard in a debate: Greece vs Rome. Johnson took the Greek side, while Beard took the Roman side.

Johnson made passionate arguments against Rome. He asked ,"What did the Romans do to democracy my friends?" , he answered ,"They abolished it!, in favour of a dictatorship". He mentioned how Romans liked the gladiatorial games, while Greeks preferred theatre. He called the Romans – bastards.

Mary Beard made arguments in favour of Rome, like that Romans were the first people to debate the limits of political liberty and that Rome was the only place in the ancient world where the state took responsibility for ensuring its citizens had enough to eat.

It was a lively debate. Both sides made good arguments. In the end, the public voted 56% for Rome and 44% for Greece.

It was a sign of the things to come.

Around the same time, the Conservative government under David Cameron agreed to hold a referendum whether Britain should stay or leave the European Union.

You could argue that it was something similar if 2000 years ago, the Roman Imperial Government allowed the citizens of Roman Greece to vote whether they want to stay or leave Rome.

Johnson had to think which side he should endorse- Leave or Remain. In February 2016, he chose Leave.

He chose that Greece should leave Rome.

Chapter 2: Childhood of Alexander the Great

In his youth, the son of Philip II, Alexander received a rich education from the great philosopher Aristotle. He taught Alexander about logic, morals, religion, medicine, art and philosophy.

He also gave Alexander a passion of the works written by Homer. The *Iliad* became one of his favourites and he was especially fond of the character of Achilles.

Alexander the Great would go on to become a legendary figure, conquering the Persian Achaemenid Empire and some of modern India.

Boris Johnson also received good education. He studied at European School, Brussels I, Ashdown House, and Eton College. In Oxford University, he studied Classics and learned Ancient Greek and Latin.

But unlike Alexander, his rise to power would not happen as quickly.

Chapter 3: Telegraph

The newspaper Daily Telegraph has a rich history. In 1908, Kaiser Wilhelm II of Germany gave a controversial interview and called English ,"mad as March hares". It damaged Anglo-German relations.

It was there that Johnson got employed in 1994 and became a Brussels Correspondent. He wanted to appeal to the middle-class England and became a well-known Eurosceptic.

The retired British Prime Minister Margaret Thatcher enjoyed his articles, while the current Prime Minister at the time John Major view the oppositely. He even considered vetoing his candidacy as a Conservative candidate in elections for the House of Commons.

He lost to a Labour candidate in 1997 UK parliamentary elections, but in 2001 was elected as MP for Henley. It was in the middle of Tony Blair's premiership. Nobody could foresee the Age of Johnson.

Things changed after 9/11. In October, 2001, USA and allies invaded Afghanistan. After that, the President of Iraq, Saddam Hussein was wrongly accused of having weapons of mass destruction.

Some European countries, like France and Germany opposed the invasion. United Kingdom was not one of them. MP Boris Johnson voted with the governments plans to support the invasion. Interestingly, the opposition Conservative party voted 146-2 for the invasion, while the Labour MP's where much more divided, voting 254-84 in favour. Nevertheless, the government's motion won, and UK helped USA in the invasion. In April 2003, Johnson visited occupied Baghdad. In 2006, Johnson called the invasion ,"a colossal mistake".

In 2008, Johnsons career received a significant boost when he was elected as Mayor of London.

Chapter 5: Athens

One of the most famous people in Ancient Greek history is Pericles. During the mid-5th century BCE, he was in charge of the city-state of Athens. At the time, Athens was one of the two most powerful Greek states, the other one being Sparta.

Under Pericles, Athens enjoyed its Golden Age and it is now even called the Age of Pericles. He fostered Athenian democracy and reconstructed major Greek temples like the Parthenon.

The major Greek playwrights like Aeschylus, Sophocles and Euripides lived during that era, as well as he historians Herodotus and Thucydides, philosophers Socrates and Plato and also the great physician Hippocrates.

Major things happened in London under Mayor Johnson: 2012 Olympic Games, although it was mostly a project of the previous Mayor Kevin Livingstone, whom Johnson defeated in 2008.

Johnson, although a controversial Mayor, was seen by some as a man of the people. He supported London Living Wage and introduced a public bicycle scheme, which proved to be very popular. They became known as "Boris Bikes".

During his time in office, in 2011 London Riots occurred, but did not bring down Johnson.

Pericles rule ended tragically. In 431 BCE, war with Sparta began, which became known as the Peloponnesian War. In 429 BCE, Pericles succumbed to the Plague of Athens and died, while Athens surrendered to Sparta in 404 BCE and the war ended in Athenian defeat.

Johnson's rule as Mayor ended differently. In 2012 he was re-elected. It was in his second term-2015, that the great debate between Mary Beard and him took place. Johnson chose not run for a third term in 2016, leaving office as a very popular mayor.

Before that, in 2015 UK parliamentary elections, Johnson was elected as an MP for Uxbridge and South Ruislip, therefore he still remained an important public figure.

But by 2016, he was a much more important figure than he was when he was first elected in 2001 and the political situation in UK was also much different.

The Brexit debate was going strong before and after his 2016 February endorsement of Leave – endorsement of Greece.

Bust of Pericles

None of the Roman Emperors ever allowed Greece to vote itself out of Rome, neither did the Sultans of the Turkish Ottoman Empire, but it was able to fight for its independence and won in a war of independence which lasted from 1821 to 1829. Greece was free.

In 2016, it was United Kingdom which was fighting for its independence from the European Union- the Brexiters argued. Johnson was one of those Brexiters.

When Greece was fighting the Ottomans, they received international support from Russia, France and the United Kingdom. When Britain was doing so, it was quite the opposite. The major countries of the world supported Remain. In April 2016, President Barack Obama made comments supporting the remain side. Johnson criticized him for it. Naturally the governments of Germany and France also supported Remain, being the major countries of the EU.

The majority of the Greeks probably, being not big fans of EU supported Leave. But in the end, it was the British people who had to decide.

Chapter 7: Victory

The day of 23rd of June, 2016 was a day of victory. It was both like a victory in a war, and a revolution combined in one. Johnson argued that the day should become ''Britain's Independence Day''.

Prime Minister David Cameron announced his resignation. Johnson was seen as a front-runner to succeed him. However, another Brexiter Michael Gove said that Johnson ,''cannot provide the leadership or build the team for the task ahead'' and announced his candidacy. Quickly after that, Johnson announced that he was not running. But Gove only received a distant third place in Conservative Leadership Election. Home Secretary Theresa May, who supported Remain was elected the new Conservative leader and became Prime Minister.

Brexit won, but Johnson did not, but neither did he lose. Prime Minister May appointed him as the new Foreign Secretary, although the posts of the International Trade Secretary and the newly created Brexit Secretary would have been more favourable to him. Some saw this as an attempt to weaken Johnson.

Chapter 8: Exile

The post of Foreign Secretary requires a lot of travelling. Therefore it was not Johnson who was dealing with Brexit.

It was Theresa May. At first, she was quite a popular Prime Minister, even with staunch Brexiters, enjoying a long honeymoon and triggering Article 50 which increased her popularity.

Having high ratings in election opinion polls, she called an election, which after a bad campaign lost her majority. Democratic Unionist Party (DUP) agreed to support May's government.

May continued as Prime Minister, while in July 2018, seeing May as too much collaborative with the EU, Johnson resigned his post, along with Brexit secretary David Davis. Exile, began, but it would only last a year.

Chapter 9: Comeback

Winston Churchill had a long and known 10-year exile from 1929 to 1939, which are known as his wilderness years.

Johnson only had one year of wilderness, although even in the middle of his first year in the wilderness, he became more important, while Theresa May started to lose her power.

After her deal was defeated three times in the House of Commons, delaying Brexit to April 12, 2019 and then to October 31, 2019 , and after she mentioned the possibility of a second referendum, her power within the party completely evaporated and she announced her resignation on 24th of May, fully resigning after a successor was elected.

The European Parliament Elections in UK held on 23rd of May, 2019 resulted in a big victory for Nigel Farage's Brexit Party receiving 30.5% , while the Conservatives only received a 5th place with 8.8%.

The Conservative Party's support in the opinion polls for a next national election dropped drastically, while the Brexit Party in some polls even topped into a first place. The Conservatives needed a saviour and they needed one quickly.

Even before May's resignation, Johnson on May 16th announced that he would stand for leadership of the Conservative Party. He launched his campaign on 7th of June and after winning every ballot, he was elected as the new leader of the Conservative Party on 22nd of July, 2019, assumed the leadership of the party on 23rd of July and the premiership of 24th of July. The Age of Johnson had begun.

Chapter 10: Age of Johnson

Age of Johnson began victoriously for Prime Minister Boris Johnson, but soon doubts began to emerge how long it would last.

On 28th of August, Prime Minister Johnson announced that he asked the Queen to prorogue the Parliament from around 10th of September which would have lasted until 14th of October. Immediately he was showing strong leadership.

On 3rd of September, Phillip Lee crossed the floor and defected to the Liberal Democrats following disagreement with Johnson's Brexit policy. This left the government with no working majority in the House of Commons.

Soon after, Benn Act was passed preventing a no deal for 31st of October. 21 Conservative members voted for the act and as a result, they lost their whip, making it harder for the government to attain a majority.

Benn Act forced Johnson to ask EU for a delay if he did not get a new deal or if the House of Commons failed to agree to one. Some speculated that Johnson would ignore this law and not ask for an extension, leading a possible imprisonment, which would have led to a sudden end of the Age of Johnson.

But that did not happen.

During that time, Prime Minister Johnson also failed to win support for a snap election.

Later the prorogation was declared unlawful by the UK Supreme Court and the parliament returned the following day.

Many blame him for loosing so many votes in the House, but as he was leading a minority government, it was quite hard to win votes.

Chapter 11: Age of Johnson Continues

On the 17th of October, Prime Minister Johnson and the European Union agreed to a new deal. However, MPs passed an amendment, introduced by Sir Oliver Letwin by 322 votes to 306, withholding Parliament's approval until legislation implementing the deal has been passed, and forced the Government to request the EU for a delay to Brexit until 31 January 2020.

On the 22nd of October, the new deal was passed by 329-299 votes, marking a significant achievement of Johnson premiership, however timetable for debating the Bill, was defeated by 322 votes to 308.

Prime Minister Boris Johnson sent a letter for EU (not written by him) asking for an extension and the letter written by him recommending not to give one. Others argue that he broke his promise, which was for UK to leave on 31st of October, but they forget that he was bound by law to do so.

EU agreed to delay Brexit to 31st of January, making it possible to leave earlier when all arrangements are decided. (Flextension).

Chapter 12: The future for the Age of Johnson

Prime Minister Boris Johnson agreed to ask EU for another Brexit delay, which got rid of the talk of an imprisonment if he did not ask for one. Therefore, the first threat to the Age of Johnson was removed, but the future of it is still uncertain.

On 29th of October, British MP's agreed to a new election, to be held on 12th of December, 2019, making it the first winter election since 1923.

Prime Minister Boris Johnson was heavily criticized for his actions, since he became Prime Minister, more strongly than many other previous Prime Ministers. Many opposition figures called him to resign or be removed from office.

But this has not translated into public opinion. He has restored the position of the Conservative Party in election opinion polls, restoring it from the 17% it had in June, 2019 to 41% it now had in October, 2019.

There is still campaigning to do. Prime Minister Boris Johnson has ruled out a coalition with the Nigel Farage's Brexit Party as that would be quite improbable, due to Johnson's new deal he got which again increased his popularity and Brexit Party's strong opposition to the deal and support of no deal.

What will happen on 12th of December is yet uncertain, but if Johnson wins, the Age of Johnson could last a long time, maybe even a decade.

Usually successful Prime Ministers considered by historians have a hard start, but they deal with it and become successful leaders.

Prime Minister Boris Johnson has already dealt with many challenges successfully in his premiership, the main one being the deal getting passed by UK parliament and improving his party's standing in the polls, therefore the future for Prime Minister Boris Johnson and the Age of Johnson is still uncertain, but there is a possibility that it will be bright.

Some Remainers unhappy with 2016 result will continuously campaign for a second referendum or for revoking Article 50, but Prime Minister Boris Johnson will not allow that to happen. He will fight for a free Britain, the one which is not a member of the European Union.

He will fight for a free Greece, both from Rome and from the Ottomans!

THE END